WORLD'S GREATEST G
FOR PIANO & VOICE

70 GOSPEL FAVORITES
Arranged with a Piano Accompaniment that is
also complete in itself for Solo Performance
Includes Vocal Line, Lyrics and Guitar Chords

Selected and Arranged by
JERRY RAY

World's Greatest Gospel Songs contains some of the most uplifting, powerful and emotion-ally-charged songs of all time. One of the special characteristics of gospel music is its ability to evoke a variety of reactions from the listener. At times, gospel music can be fun, upbeat and happy. It's the perfect addition to the excitement of a good ol' fashioned camp meeting where foot stamping, hand clapping and shouts of "amen" abound. At other times, gospel music can tell a story so sad, painful and solemn that it tears your heart to pieces. But gospel music is *always* about the *good news*—the good news of love, forgive-ness, refreshment, joy, redemption and release. Each song has been carefully arranged with a very accessible approach, and features:

- an introduction in the same style as the song's setting
- a vocal line for solo or group singing
- an appropriately selected key to accommodate a comfortable vocal range
- up to three verses of lyrics
- a first and second ending with an appropriate "turnaround," plus a final ending that complements the musical style of the arrangement
- guitar chords
- dynamics
- a piano accompaniment that is complete in itself for solo performance

For decades, gospel music has been used to bring the good news to the far reaches of the planet. It can move mountains. It can bring ecstatic jubilation. It can calm the storm. It can bring a grown man to tears. And it can bring a quiet peace that lasts a lifetime. Above all, my hope is that in some way *World's Greatest Gospel Songs* will help bring you both quiet peace *and* ecstatic jubilation just when life's mountains seem to jump right in front of you. Now turn the page and get ready for a little foot stamping, hand clapping and shouts of "amen!"

Sing on!

Jerry Ray

Alfred

2

TABLE OF CONTENTS

Amazing Grace

Words by John Newton

Traditional melody
Arranged by Jerry Ray

At Calvary

Words by William R. Newell

Music by Daniel B. Towner
Arranged by Jerry Ray

1. Years I spend in van - i - ty and pride, car - ing not my Lord was
2. By God's Word at last my sin I learned, then I trem - bled at the
3. Oh, the love that drew sal - va - tion's plan! Oh, the grace that brought it

cru - ci - fied, know - ing not it was for me He died on
law I'd spurned, till my guilt - y soul im - plor - ing turned to
down to man! Oh, the might - y gulf that God did span at

At the Cross

Words by Isaac Watts

Music by Ralph E. Hudson
Arranged by Jerry Ray

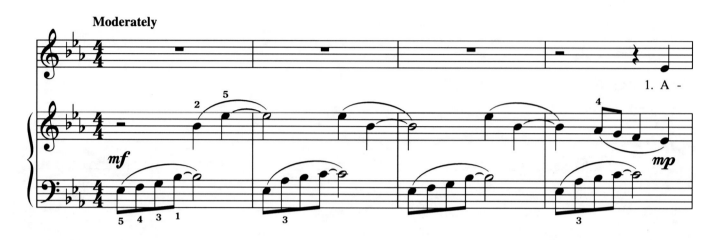

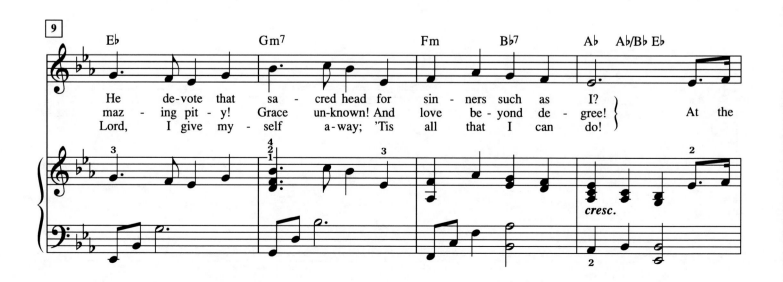

Battle Hymn of the Republic

Words by Julia Ward Howe

Music by William Steffe
Arranged by Jerry Ray

Blessed Be the Name

Words by William H. Clark
and Ralph E. Hudson

Music by Ralph E. Hudson
Arranged by Jerry Ray

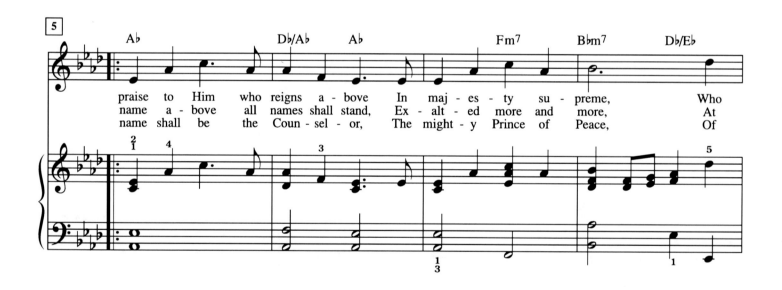

praise to Him who reigns a - bove In maj - es - ty su - preme, Who
name a - bove all names shall stand, Ex - alt - ed more and more, At
name shall be the Coun - sel - or, The might - y Prince of Peace, Of

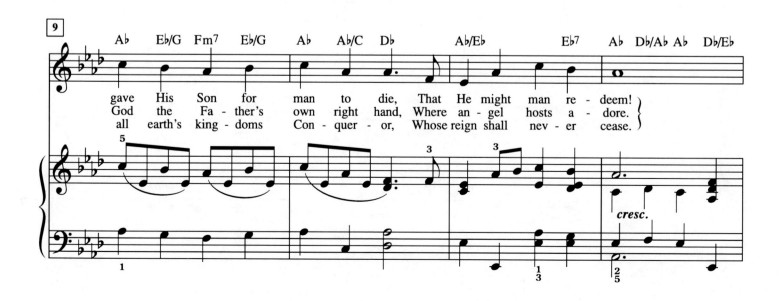

gave His Son for man to die, That He might man re - deem!
God the Fa - ther's own right hand, Where an - gel hosts a - dore.
all earth's king - doms Con - quer - or, Whose reign shall nev - er cease.

Blest Be the Tie That Binds

Words by John Fawcett

Music by Johann G. Nägeli
Arranged by Jerry Ray

Brighten the Corner Where You Are

Words by Ina Dudley Ogdon

Music by Charles H. Gabriel
Arranged by Jerry Ray

Church in the Wildwood

Words by William S. Pitts

Music by William S. Pitts
Arranged by Jerry Ray

Count Your Blessings

Words by Johnson Oatman, Jr.

Music by Edwin O. Excell
Arranged by Jerry Ray

Do, Lord

Traditional
Arranged by Jerry Ray

Does Jesus Care?

Words by Frank E. Graeff

Music by J. Lincoln Hall
Arranged by Jerry Ray

Down at the Cross

Words by Elisha A. Hoffman

Music by John H. Stockton
Arranged by Jerry Ray

Dwelling in Beulah Land

Words by C. Austin Miles

Music by C. Austin Miles
Arranged by Jerry Ray

liv-ing on the moun-tain, un-der-neath a cloud-less sky, I'm drink-ing at the foun-tain that

nev-er shall run dry; O yes! I'm feast-ing on the man-na from a boun-ti-ful sup-ply, For I am

dwell-ing in Beu-lah Land._____ Land.

Footsteps of Jesus

Words by Mary B. C. Slade

Music by Asa B. Everett
Arranged by Jerry Ray

1. Sweet - ly, Lord, have we heard Thee call - ing,
2. If they lead through the tem - ple ho - ly,
3. Then at last when on high He sees us,

"Come, fol - low Me!" And we see where Thy
Preach - ing the Word; Or we in homes where of the
Our jour - ney done, We will rest where the

foot - prints fall - ing, Lead us to Thee.
poor and low - ly, serv - ing the Lord.
steps of Je - sus end at His throne.

Give Me That Old Time Religion

Traditional
Arranged by Jerry Ray

God Is So Good

Traditional
Arranged by Jerry Ray

God Leads Us Along

Words by George A. Young

Music by George A. Young
Arranged by Jerry Ray

God Will Take Care of You

Words by Civilla D. Martin

Music by W. Stillman Martin
Arranged by Jerry Ray

1. Be not dis-mayed what-e'er be-tide;
2. All you may need He will pro-vide;
3. No mat-ter what may be the test,

God will take care of you. Be-neath His wings of
God will take care of you. Noth-ing you ask will
God will take care of you. Lean, wea-ry one, up-

love a-bide; God will take care of you.
be de-nied; God will take care of you.
on His breast; God will take care of you.

Hallelujah, We Shall Rise

Words by John E. Thomas

Music by John E. Thomas
Arranged by Jerry Ray

1. In the res-ur-rec-tion morn-ing, when the
res-ur-ec-tion morn-ing, what a
res-ur-ec-tion morn-ing, we shall

trump of God shall sound, We shall rise, hal - le - lu - jah! we shall
meet - ing it will be! We shall rise, hal - le - lu - jah! we shall
meet Him in the air. We shall rise, hal - le - lu - jah! we shall

rise!
rise!
rise!

Then the saints will come re - joic-ing and no tears will e'er be found.
When our fa - thers and our moth-ers and our loved ones we shall see! } We shall
And be car - ried up to glo - ry, to our home so bright and fair.

The Haven of Rest

Words by Henry L. Gilmour

Music by George D. Moore
Arranged by Jerry Ray

He Hideth My Soul

Words by Fanny J. Crosby

Music by William J. Kirkpatrick
Arranged by Jerry Ray

1. A won-der-ful Sav-ior is Je-sus my Lord, A
   won-der-ful Sav-ior is Je-sus my Lord, He
   clothed in His bright-ness, trans-port-ed I rise To

won-der-ful Sav-ior to me;___ He hid-eth my soul in the
tak-eth my bur-den a-way;___ He hold-eth me up, and I
meet Him in clouds of the sky,___ His per-fect sal-va-tion, His

cleft of the rock, Where riv-ers of pleas-ure I see.___ He
shall not be moved; He giv-eth me strength as my day.___ He
won-der-ful love I'll shout with the mil-lions on high!

Heavenly Sunlight

Words by Henry J. Zelley

Music by George Harrison Cook
Arranged by Jerry Ray

He's Got the Whole World in His Hands

Traditional
Arranged by Jerry Ray

Higher Ground

Words by Johnson Oatman, Jr.

Music by Charles H. Gabriel
Arranged by Jerry Ray

Highway to Heaven

Words by Rev. Thomas A. Dorsey

Music by Rev. Thomas A. Dorsey
Arranged by Jerry Ray

Moderately

It's a

high - way to Heav - en, None can walk up there but the pure in heart; It's a

high - way to Heav - en, Walk-ing up the King's high - way;

1. My way is bright-er, my load is light-er, Walk-ing up the King's high - way;
2. If you're not walk-ing, start while I'm talk-ing, Walk-ing up the King's high - way;

His Eye Is on the Sparrow

Words by Civilla D. Martin

Music by Charles H. Gabriel
Arranged by Jerry Ray

How Beautiful Heaven Must Be

Words by Mrs. A. S. Bridgewater

Music by A. P. Bland
Arranged by Jerry Ray

I Am Thine, O Lord

Words by Fanny Crosby

Music by William Howard Doane
Arranged by Jerry Ray

I Have Decided to Follow Jesus

Traditional
Arranged by Jerry Ray

I Must Tell Jesus

Words by Elisha A. Hoffman

Music by Elisha A. Hoffman
Arranged by Jerry Ray

I Will Sing of My Redeemer

Words by Philip P. Bliss

Music by James McGranahan
Arranged by Jerry Ray

I'm So Glad Jesus Lifted Me

Traditional
Arranged by Jerry Ray

In the Garden

Words by C. Austin Miles

Music by C. Austin Miles
Arranged by Jerry Ray

I've Got Peace Like a River

Traditional
Arranged by Jerry Ray

Jesus Is the Sweetest Name I Know

Words by Lela B. Long

Music by Lela B. Long
Arranged by Jerry Ray

Jesus Loves Me

Words by Anna B. Warner

Music by William B. Bradbury
Arranged by Jerry Ray

Jesus Loves the Little Children

Words by Rev. C. Herbert Woolston

Music by George F. Root
Arranged by Jerry Ray

With a bounce

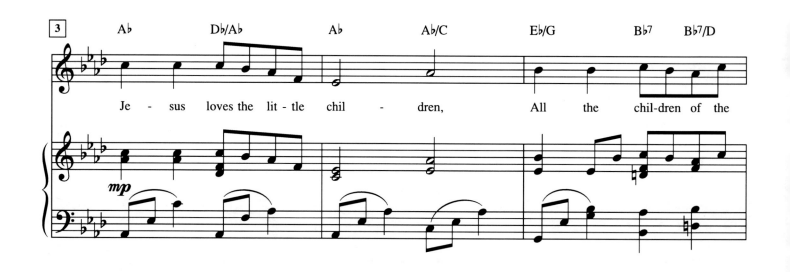

Je - sus loves the lit - tle chil - dren, All the chil-dren of the

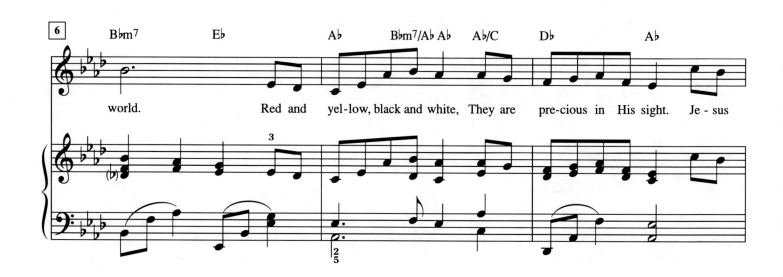

world. Red and yel-low, black and white, They are pre-cious in His sight. Je - sus

Jesus Saves!

Words by Priscilla J. Owens

Music by William J. Kirkpatrick
Arranged by Jerry Ray

Joshua Fit the Battle of Jericho

Spiritual
Arranged by Jerry Ray

Just a Closer Walk with Thee

Traditional
Arranged by Jerry Ray

Kum Ba Yah

Traditional
Arranged by Jerry Ray

Let Us Break Bread Together

Spiritual
Arranged by Jerry Ray

The Lily of the Valley

Words by Charles W. Fry

Music by William S. Hayes
Arranged by Jerry Ray

Lord, I'm Coming Home

Words by William J. Kirkpatrick

Music by William J. Kirkpatrick
Arranged by Jerry Ray

The Love of God

Words by Frederick M. Lehman

Music by Frederick M. Lehman
Arranged by Jerry Ray

No, Not One!

Words by Johnson Oatman, Jr.

Music by George C. Hugg
Arranged by Jerry Ray

Oh, How I Love Jesus

Words by Frederick Whitfield

Traditional American Melody
Arranged by Jerry Ray

The Old Rugged Cross

Words by George Bennard

Music by George Bennard
Arranged by Jerry Ray

Precious Memories

Words by J. B. F. Wright

Music by J. B. F. Wright
Arranged by Jerry Ray

1. Pre - cious mem-'ries,__ un - seen an - gels,__ Sent from some-where to my soul; How they lin - ger,__ ev - er near me,__ And the sa - cred past un - fold.

2. Pre - cious fa - ther,__ lov - ing moth-er,__ Fly a - cross the lone-ly years; To old home scenes_ of my child-hood,__ With fond mem - o - ries ap - pear.

Rock of Ages

Words by Augustus M. Toplady

Music by Thomas Hastings
Arranged by Jerry Ray

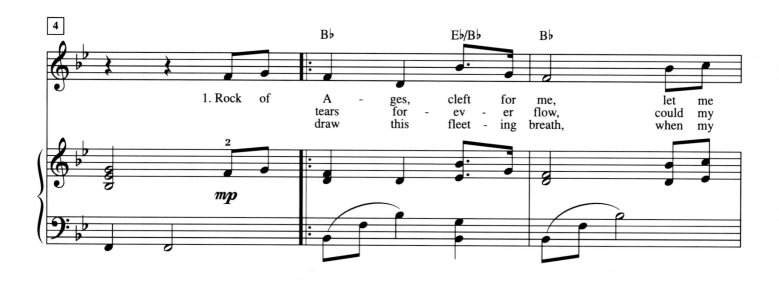

Send the Light

Words by Charles H. Gabriel

Music by Charles H. Gabriel
Arranged by Jerry Ray

Shall We Gather at the River

Words by Robert Lowry

Music by Robert Lowry
Arranged by Jerry Ray

Since Jesus Came into My Heart

Words by Rufus H. McDaniel

Music by Charles H. Gabriel
Arranged by Jerry Ray

Sweet By and By

Words by Sanford Fillmore Bennett

Music by Joseph P. Webster
Arranged by Jerry Ray

Swing Down, Chariot

Spiritual
Arranged by Jerry Ray

Swing Low, Sweet Chariot

Spiritual
Arranged by Jerry Ray

There Is Power in the Blood

Words by Lewis E. Jones

Music by Lewis E. Jones
Arranged by Jerry Ray

There Shall Be Showers of Blessing

Words by Daniel W. Whittle

Music by James McGranahan
Arranged by Jerry Ray

This Little Light of Mine

Traditional
Arranged by Jerry Ray

This World Is Not My Home

Words by S. D. Burton

Music by E. B. Graham
Arranged by Jerry Ray

To God Be the Glory

Words by Fanny J. Crosby

Music by William H. Doane
Arranged by Jerry Ray

Turn Your Eyes Upon Jesus

Words by Helen Lemmel

Music by Helen Lemmel
Arranged by Jerry Ray

Unclouded Day

Words by Josiah K. Alwood

Music by Josiah K. Alwood
Arranged by Jerry Ray

We'll Understand It Better By and By

Words by Charles A. Tindley

Music by Charles A. Tindley
Arranged by Jerry Ray

When the Roll Is Called Up Yonder

Words by James M. Black

Music by James M. Black
Arranged by Jerry Ray

When the Saints Go Marching In

Words by Katherine E. Purvis

Music by James M. Black
Arranged by Jerry Ray

When We All Get to Heaven

Words by Eliza E. Hewitt

Music by Emily D. Wilson
Arranged by Jerry Ray

1. Sing the won - drous love of Je - sus,
2. Let us then be true and faith - ful,
3. On - ward to the prize be - fore us!

Sing His mer - cy and His grace. In the man - sions
Trust - ing serv - ing ev - 'ry day; Just one glimpse of
Soon His beau - ty we'll be - hold; Soon the pearl - y

bright and bless - ed He'll pre - pare us for a place.
Him in glo - ry Will the toils of life re - pay.
gates will o - pen; We shall tread the streets of gold.

When we

Dedicated to the McMurry United Methodist Girl's Youth Trio: Jacqueline Lane-Borton, Vivian Croy-Loipersbeck
and Mary Alice Lane-Toy, as performed in Claycomo, Missouri, circa 1941

Whispering Hope

Words by Septimus Winner

Music by Septimus Winner
Arranged by Jerry Ray

1. Soft as the voice of an an - gel Breath - ing a les - son un - heard,
2. If, in the dusk of the twi - light, Dim be the re - gion a - far,
3. Hope, as an an-chor so stead - fast, Rends the dark veil for the soul,

Hope with a gen-tle per - sua - sion Whis - pers her com-fort-ing word:
Will not the deep-en - ing dark - ness Bright - en the glim-mer-ing star?
Whith - er the Mas-ter has en - tered, Rob - bing the grave of its goal.

Wait till the dark - ness is o - ver, Wait till the tem-pest is done,
Then when the night is up - on us, Why should the heart sink a - way?
Come then, O come, glad fru - i - tion, Come to my sad wea-ry heart.

Will the Circle Be Unbroken

Words by Ada R. Habershom

Music by Charles H. Gabriel
Arranged by Jerry Ray

Wonderful Grace of Jesus

Words by Haldor Lillenas

Music by Haldor Lillenas
Arranged by Jerry Ray

1. Won - der - ful grace of Je - sus, great - er than all my
2. Won - der - ful grace of Je - sus, reach - ing to all the
3. Won - der - ful grace of Je - sus, reach - ing the most de -

sin.
lost.
filed.

How shall my tongue de - scribe it,
By it I have been par - doned,
By its trans-form - ing pow - er,

where shall its praise be - gin?
saved to the ut - ter - most.
mak - ing me God's dear child.

Tak - ing a - way my
Chains have been torn a -
Pur - chas - ing peace and